INSTRUCTIONS NOT INCLUDED

How a Team of Women Coded the Future

For Julia —T.L.B.

For David —D.L.D.

For my parents, who did just fine without instructions —C.B.

Our deepest thanks to Sarah Davies, Rotem Moscovich, Heather Crowley, and Mary Claire Cruz. And special thanks to UPenn professor Mitch Marcus for his meticulous review of our manuscript. Any remaining errors are our own.

First Edition, October 2019
10 9 8 7 6 5 4 3 2 1
FAC-029191-19193
Printed in Malaysia

This book is set in New Baskerville ITC Pro/International; KG Fall For You, CLHeading, Supernett/Fontspring
Designed by Mary Claire Cruz

Library of Congress Cataloging-in-Publication Data

Names: Brown, Tami Lewis, author. • Dunn, Debbie Loren, author.
  • Beck, Chelsea, 1994- illustrator.
Title: Instructions not included : how a team of women coded the future /
  by Tami Lewis Brown and Debbie Loren Dunn ; illustrated by Chelsea Beck.
Description: First edition. • Los Angeles : Disney/Hyperion, 2019.
  • Includes bibliographical references. • Audience: Age 6-8.
Identifiers: LCCN 2018053225 • ISBN 9781368011051 (hardcover)
  • ISBN 1368011055 (hardcover)
Subjects: LCSH: Women computer scientists—United States—Biography—Juvenile
  literature. • Computer scientists—United States—Biography—Juvenile
  literature. • ENIAC (Computer)—Juvenile literature. • Bartik,
  Jean—Juvenile literature. • Mauchly-Antonelli, Kay—Juvenile literature.
  • Holberton, Frances Elizabeth—Juvenile literature.
Classification: LCC QA76.2.A2 B76 2019 • DDC 004.092—dc23
LC record available at https://lccn.loc.gov/2018053225

Reinforced binding

Visit www.DisneyBooks.com

INSTRUCTIONS NOT INCLUDED

How a Team of Women Coded the Future

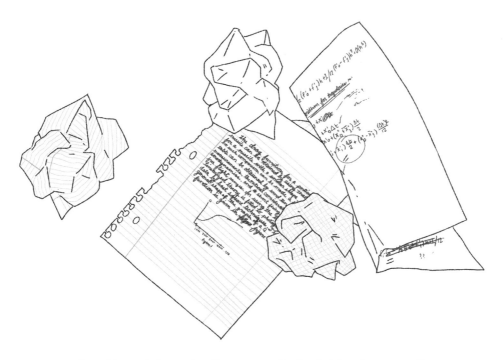

By Tami Lewis Brown & Debbie Loren Dunn

Illustrated by Chelsea Beck

Disney · HYPERION

Los Angeles   New York

Not so long ago, there were no computers.

Math problems were solved with pencil and paper.

Telephones, with rotary dials, were tethered to wires.

Mail arrived in an envelope, carried by a postman.

Files were stored in paper folders and metal cabinets.

All that work took lots of steps,
and lots of people, and lots of time.

But some people thought
there was a better way—
an automatic way—
to solve routine problems
by using a machine.

Three computer pioneers—

and their computer, ENIAC:

a computer like Betty, different from anything anybody had ever seen,

like Jean, persistent and consistent,

like Kay, no mistakes, every answer perfect—

a computer programmed to perform like the women who made it,

and like computers still perform today.

This is their story.

It's the 1930s.

Left-handed Betty,
out of place,
stands on the wrong side
of her double bass.
The conductor scolds.

Make it sound silky. Make it bellow deep.
Cross-eyed, bullied, and teased,
she plucks the strings with stubborn zeal.
Betty Snyder plays her own way.

Farm girl Jean, tall and lean,
winds up and rocks back.
Her softball hits the side of the barn.

A thousand tosses, a thousand throws,
a thousand pitches.
Until every ball strikes the tiny tin target.
Jean Jennings aims to win.

A+ Kay, never misses a day.

She skips third grade, on up to fourth.

Her pencil pirouettes, eraser confetti flies.

Perfect attendance, perfect report cards, perfect behavior.

Even a prize for perfect handwriting.

Kay McNulty curtsies to the crowd.

Betty, Jean, and Kay
do not know one another.

Not yet.

But, in her sleep, Betty dreams of music and equations.

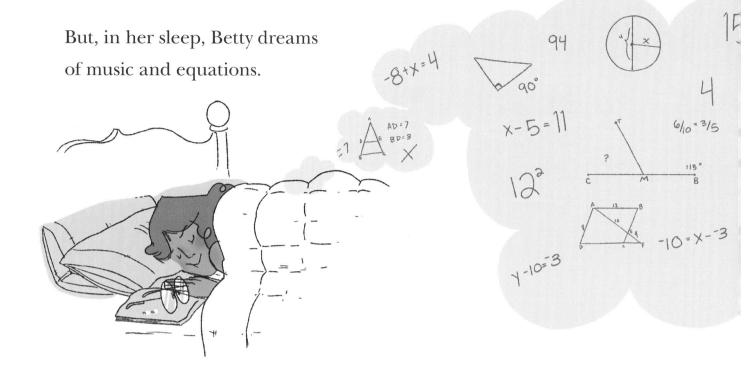

While in a one-room schoolhouse, Jean masters fifth-, sixth-, and seventh-grade math, all in one year.

And in her Irish accent, Kay tutors her big brothers:
first English, then poetry, and then, of course, arithmetic.

The girls are brilliant, brave, and bold.
But best of all,

they love math.

Now it is 1944.

The world is at war.
All hands on deck, America calls.

At a secret lab at the University of Pennsylvania,
a hundred women, called "computers,"
solve tens of thousands of math problems,
using only paper, pencils,
and adding machines.

Which angle to aim a gun and
when to launch a bomb.
They calculate around the clock,
to win the war with math.

But upstairs there's a bigger secret,
a top secret,
a secret weapon.

Upstairs,

circuits are soldered,

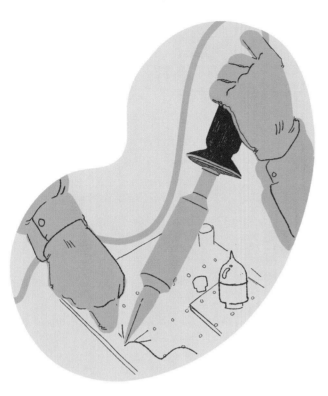

panels built,

cables strung,

and switches wired.

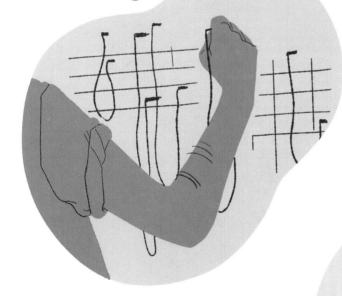

Upstairs, a machine is being born,
one that will do the work of all the
human computers in a fraction of the time.

The machine's name is ENIAC.

It weighs thirty tons, and it's one hundred feet long.
Some say, when they switch ENIAC on,
the lights of Philadelphia dim.

It will take more than one mind to
realize a dream as big as ENIAC.
It will take engineers
and electricians,
machinists

and mathematicians.

A half dozen mathematicians, including
Betty, Jean, and Kay, are invited upstairs
to solve some of the most complicated
problems anyone has ever faced—
to invent a way to tell a machine to
perform complex calculations
at record speeds,
and to make sure its answers
are always correct.

ENIAC comes with no guidelines or rules.
INSTRUCTIONS NOT INCLUDED.
And at first, the women aren't allowed to
touch, or even see, the computer.
Still, the bosses shout

Engineers solder circuit boards and machinists forge frames—
and Betty, Jean, and Kay begin, too,

adding,

subtracting,

multiplying,

dividing,

translating math's logic into a code that
will command ENIAC to perform.

As the mighty machine comes together,
and electricity and data begin to flow . . .
the team now toggle hundreds of switches
on ENIAC's front, plug countless tubes into its back,
and string miles of wire between the panels.

They sing and dance and calculate
around the clock,
until they fall asleep.

Finally, Betty, Jean, and Kay are ordered to unveil ENIAC

to dignitaries, generals, and even their own bosses.

In two weeks' time, they are expected

to demonstrate ENIAC's speed and power,

to prove this machine is worthy
of the huge investment,
and to show that computers
have a future,
in war and in peace.

With a massive stack of punch cards,
Betty, Jean, and Kay send information to the computer
and program ENIAC for its debut.

It's a complicated test problem—an artillery launch—with many variables,
like air temperature,
altitude,
weight,
and speed,
all calculated in a flash,
with just one chance to hit the target.

And ENIAC
isn't ready.

While Betty and Jean
pitch ideas, untangle logical knots,
and imagine solutions,
above and beyond,
Kay checks the calculations
the old-fashioned way,
with pencil and paper.

Kay's answers are always right.
But can ENIAC
perform as well?

Or will it stumble?
Project canceled.
Expensive machine scrapped.
Brilliant mathematicians sent home.
Ending it all . . .
for the world's fastest computer and
for Betty and Jean and Kay.

The women set up the problem.

Click　　　　　　　*Whir*　　　　　　　*Buzz*

ENIAC spits out the result.

Answer: WRONG.

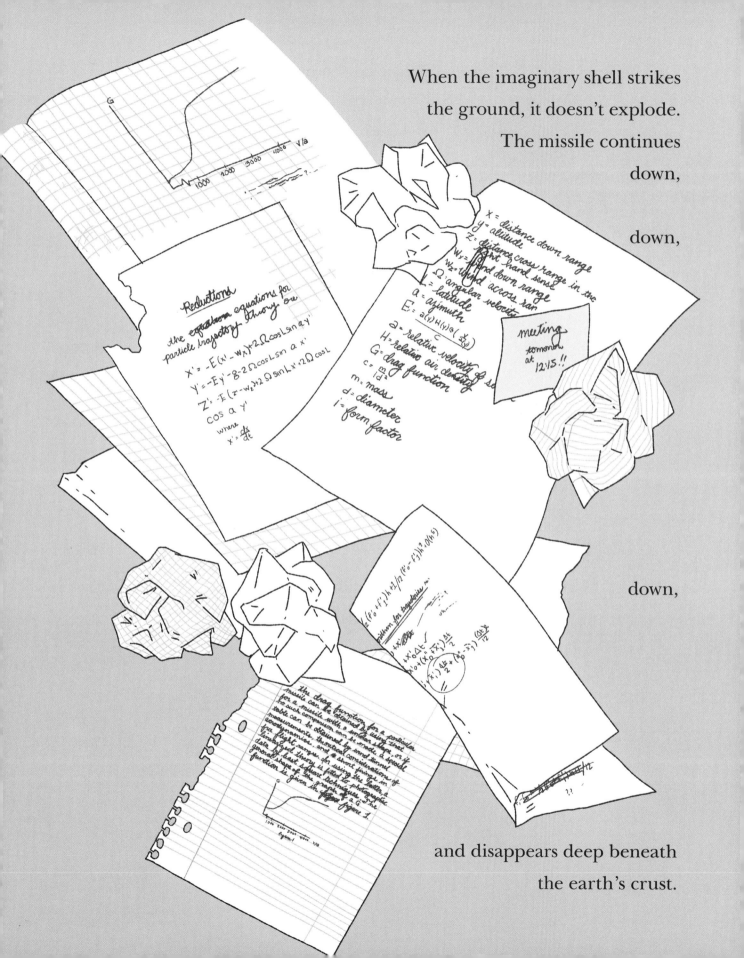

When the imaginary shell strikes
the ground, it doesn't explode.
The missile continues
down,

down,

down,

and disappears deep beneath
the earth's crust.

Betty and Jean reanalyze. Kay recalculates.

Readjust. Rework. Reprogram.

Then start all over again.

Click   *Whir*   *Buzz*

Click   *Whir*   *Buzz*

But ENIAC is still WRONG.

Where is the trouble?

Where is the bug?

Tomorrow the dignitaries and generals
and bosses will march in, and
ENIAC's answer will still be WRONG!

But the women and their computer can't fail.

Not now.

Not with so much at stake.

They recalculate, reanalyze,
and program again.

Finally, exhausted, Betty falls asleep.

But her mind is still awake.

And suddenly she dreams the solution.

ENIAC's program is repeating one of the calculations.

ENIAC and the bomb don't know when to stop!

So the women toggle a single switch—out of thousands—

to change the equation.

Then they take a deep, deep breath.

The next morning, the dignitaries and generals and bosses march in.

Arms fold, lips purse, brows wrinkle.

Click   *Whir*   *Buzz*

Click Click Click

Click.

Out shoots a keypunch card
with the answer. . . .

The dignitaries and generals and bosses congratulate themselves.

GOOD JOB!

GREAT SHOW!

The men shake each other's hands.

WE'VE DONE IT!

And they march out for their celebration banquet.

But there are no congratulations for the programmers.

The women and ENIAC celebrate alone.

Still, the next day, and the next, and the next . . .

and the next,

Betty and Jean and Kay keep programming.

To solve the biggest problems,

computer memory has to be elegantly organized,

as carefully composed as a symphony.

Betty arranges computer memory in logical harmony.

Now the machine sifts data with a single command.

Her innovation is called SORT-MERGE.

To repeat a procedure without moving the machine's wires,

a computer must remember and replay.

Jean makes computers hold their instructions,

like a star pitcher whose arm has a memory of its own.

Her innovation is called a **STORED PROGRAM.**

To make computers faster, smaller, and more powerful,
they must do more with less.
Kay shuffles the code so
computers are smart and thrifty.

Her innovation is called **REDUCING** and **REUSING MEMORY**.

Betty, Jean, and Kay unleash their talents,
share their secrets,
pair their smarts with the computer's speed.

Exploring. Creating. Inventing.

Using math in a way that nobody had ever dreamed of,

unraveling problems that no one had ever solved before,

until ENIAC is not the only computer,

or even the fastest computer . . .

. . . until the whole world
is different and new,
and an entire computer age is born.

AUTHORS' NOTE

ENIAC, short for Electronic Numerical Integrator and Computer, was one of the first electronic computers. A thousand times faster than its closest competitor, ENIAC was a powerful but flexible tool for problem-solving because of Betty's, Jean's, and Kay's innovations. It performed a variety of tasks, from keeping track of company payrolls to running computations for the hydrogen bomb. The women's groundbreaking contributions to computer science live on in modern computers, from the most sophisticated mainframe to tiny gadgets we take for granted.

Frances Elizabeth "Betty" Snyder Holberton was born on March 7, 1917, in Philadelphia, Pennsylvania. Her first math professor at the University of Pennsylvania said that women should be home raising children instead of solving equations. Betty did both. Married with two daughters, Betty went on to work with Grace Hopper, one of the inventors of the computer language called COBOL, and played a crucial role in developing a

The women programmers set up a problem by plugging cables into ENIAC's panels. (Alamy Stock Photo)

new computer language, FORTRAN. A computer language is the way in which a person communicates what instructions or operations they want a computer

Jean Jennings Bartik and Frances Bilas operate ENIAC's main control panel. (U.S. Army)

to perform. After ENIAC's cables and switches, computers were programmed with binary code or assembly language—it was all "1's" and "0's." With the invention of COBOL and FORTRAN, the instructions were simpler to understand; terms such as ADD and SUBTRACT and PERFORM became commonplace. Betty also contributed to a groundbreaking invention called the sorting algorithm, which is used in many computer programs and apps today.

Throughout her long life, Betty always considered things anew. She designed a control panel that added numbers alongside the letters that were already there; she saw that numbers and letters belonged together. Her invention was the precursor to the keypad on keyboards we use today. Betty Holberton died in 2001.

Betty "Jean" Jennings Bartik was born in Gentry County, Missouri, on December 27, 1924. She dreamed of adventure and of leaving her small town with its one-room schoolhouse. After she graduated from Northwest Missouri State Teacher's College with a degree in mathematics, Jean's calculus teacher gave her career advice: "Go to U. of Penn; it has a differential analyzer." And she did just that. Among many accolades that she later received, Northwest Missouri State University named its computer museum in Jean's honor, and the default theme for Drupal computing—a progressive framework used to build many current websites—is called Bartik.

As part of the ENIAC project, and afterward at Eckert-Mauchly Computer Corporation, Jean, the team player, led a group that developed stored programming. Their work led to the ability of later versions of ENIAC and its descendants to hold

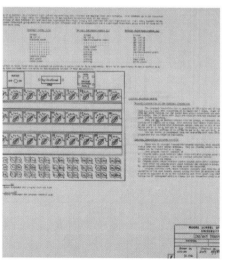

The women received stacks of electrical schematics, but there were no instructions on how to program math problems into ENIAC. (Smithsonian Libraries)

all equations in memory. The longest lived of the three women, Jean spoke on panels and gave presentations to introduce the accomplishments of this amazing team of women programmers to the digital world. Jean Bartik died in 2011.

Kathleen "Kay" McNulty Mauchly Antonelli was born in Donegal, Ireland, on February 12, 1921, during the war of Irish independence. When Kay and her family immigrated to America in 1924, they spoke only Gaelic. The experience of bridging languages and cultures must have helped Kay teach computers to communicate

Left: Betty Snyder Holberton and a technician prepare the massive machine for work. (U.S. Army)

Below: On January 30, 1942, this classified ad, seeking female mathematicians to calculate weapons trajectories, appeared in a Philadelphia newspaper. Betty, Jean, and Kay answered the call.

with humans. A frugal perfectionist, she took a bus and subway, and then walked the last mile every day to high school. She taught herself English using her brother's schoolbooks, and went on to win a scholarship to Chestnut Hill College.

After her work with the ENIAC team, Kay married John Mauchly, the physicist who, along with J. Presper Eckert, had designed and built ENIAC. Kay resigned her post to raise Mauchly's two children from a previous marriage, and then they had five more children of their own. Kay Mauchly died in 2006.

Dozens of "forgotten" women, whose efforts were key to the development of computers and technology, deserve to be celebrated. There were other important women ENIAC programmers, including Frances Bilas Spence, Ruth Lichterman Teitelbaum, and Marlyn Wescoff Meltzer. However, Betty's, Jean's, and Kay's individual innovations are long-lasting and groundbreaking. Modern computers are formed in their images.

OTHER RESOURCES

Women have always excelled at science and technology, even though their stories have sometimes been ignored or erased. Learn more by reading the following:

Robinson, Fiona. *Ada's Ideas: The Story of Ada Lovelace, the World's First Computer Programmer.* New York: Abrams, 2016.

Stanley, Diane and Jessie Hartland. *Ada Lovelace, Poet of Science: The First Computer Programmer.* New York: Simon & Schuster/Paula Wiseman, 2016.

Thimmesh, Catherine and Melissa Sweet. *Girls Think of Everything: Stories of Ingenious Inventions by Women.* Boston: Houghton Mifflin, 2000.

Wallmark, Laurie. *Grace Hopper: Queen of Computer Code.* New York: Sterling Children's Books, 2017.

Learn to code it yourself:

Liukas, Linda. *Hello Ruby: Adventures in Coding.* New York: Feiwel & Friends, 2015.

To learn more about their work, watch Kay, Jean, and Betty in these films:

The Computers: The Remarkable Story of the ENIAC Programmers. Produced by Kathy Kleiman. Vimeo, 2013.

The Queen of Code. Directed by Gillian Jacobs. FiveThirtyEight, 2015. http://fivethirtyeight.com/features/the-queen-of-code/

Top Secret Rosies: The Female "Computers" of WWII. Directed by LeAnn Erickson. Distributed by PBS, 2010. DVD.